IN BELFAST TOWN

EARLY PHOTOGRAPHS FROM THE LAWRENCE COLLECTION

1864-1880

'The town of Belfast seemed to me
really to be as neat,
prosperous, and handsome a city as need be seen.
It looks hearty, thriving and prosperous, as if
it had money in its pocket and roast-beef for dinner'.

W. M. Thackery, *The Irish sketch book
and critical reviews* (London, 1846), p.289.

'The general appearance of the town
is that of a clean, thrifty, business place,
with some of the trade and manufacture of Manchester and Glasgow,
but without the smoke or dirt of either':

Black's guide to Belfast (Edinburgh, 1872), p.325.

Brian M. Walker and Hugh Dixon

THE FRIAR'S BUSH PRESS

2 In Belfast town

CONTENTS

FOUNTAIN IN THE CRYSTAL PALACE, QUEEN'S ISLAND

This magnificent fountain was a central feature in the great glass house, called the Crystal Palace, which stood on Queen's Island. Originally called Dargan's Island, the area was created from the dredgings of the new Victoria Channel in the late 1840s. The famous William Dargan from Co. Carlow was the engineer responsible for constructing the channel which allowed large ships to reach Belfast port. The island covered seventeen acres and was laid out as the People's Pleasure Park[1] It included not only a conservatory but also an amusement arcade and menagerie. During the 1850s and 1860s it attracted large numbers of Belfast citizens, especially at Easter and throughout the summer[2] During the 1870s, however, the land was taken over for shipbuilding.

A copy of this photograph was published in the proceedings of the Belfast Natural History and Philosophical Society, 1915-16, and it is believed to be the only surviving photo-view of the fountain and building[3] The central figure on the fountain is Neptune with his crown and trident. He sits on a great shell drawn by two plunging fish-horses in the centre of an elaborate basin which is supported on the tails of dolphins. The light roof structure appears to have been supported on thin cast-iron columns and both roof and walls were made of many narrow strips of glass. The lightness of the building with its abundant vegetation must have been a change for those used to the town's narrow and crowded streets.

For Sarah Emily

The Friar's Bush Press
24 College Park Avenue
Belfast 7
Published 1984
© Copyright reserved
ISBN O 946872 01 5

Book design—Spring Graphics, Saintfield.
Typesetting—Compuset, Belfast.
Halftone reproduction—Reprographics, Belfast.
Printing—Nicholson and Bass, Mallusk.

INTRODUCTION

These views make up the earliest collection of photographs yet published on Victorian Belfast. All can be dated between the mid 1860s and 1880. They come from the Lawrence Collection in the National Library of Ireland which was also the source of the illustrations in our recent book, *No mean city: Belfast 1880-1914 in the photographs of Robert French* (Belfast, 1983). They belong, however, not to the main part of this collection, which was largely the work of Robert French, but to the little used, much earlier section of stereoscopic negatives by some unknown photographer or photographers. These forty-four pictures give us a very special view of Belfast town, shortly before it became a city.

THE PHOTOGRAPHS

The photographs constitute an important historical record. Some are views of places or objects which are the only photographs of these subjects known to exist while others show buildings before later Victorian alterations. No other photographs have ever been published of the first St Patrick's Church, Donegall Street, of the original 'black man' *in situ* in front of 'Inst', or of Alfred Street Church in unaltered state. We show here Great Victoria Street railway terminus before the addition of its *porte-cochere*, the Custom House with its changing entrances, and the Ulster Hall before the building of the neighbouring linen warehouse, now called Bryson House. A couple of the photographs include rare glimpses of the single-decker Belfast tram which was phased out after 1878 and replaced by the double-decker tram.

Other photographs in the collection are unusual views of well-known subjects, such as St Anne's, Donegall Street, viewed to great advantage from Church Street. Some pictures give good images of streetscape beyond the immediate object of the photograph: for instance, the print of the Music Hall gives a nice perspective of Upper Arthur Street, while that of Donegall Square Methodist Church shows the other buildings beyond it in Donegall Square East. In a number of cases similar photographs do exist of particular subjects but only in rare publications. Two examples of this are the pictures of the fountain in the Crystal Palace on Queen's Island and St John's Church, Laganbank.

The 44 views represented here add significantly to the total number of known photographs of Belfast, before 1880. The earliest photographic image of the town was a view of the Old Long Bridge, taken in 1840 by Francis Beatty, which does not seem to have survived[1]. A copy of a calotype of the second Marquis of Donegall, 1843, is in the Ulster Museum, as is another calotype of the unveiling ceremony of the statue of the Earl of Belfast in 1855. The Linen Hall Library owns about a dozen prints of the town in the 1870s. In the biography of W. J. Barre, the architect, published in 1868, there are 6 photographs of his buildings in Belfast[2]. The Northern Bank centenary history contains an 1860 view of High Street as well as a print of the Albert Clock under construction[3]. The main Lawrence Collection in Dublin contains a number of 1870s views of Belfast, most of which were included in *No mean city*. There are a few early photographs in private hands. Clearly, therefore, these 44 views are a valuable addition to the photographic archives of Victorian Belfast.

The photographs in this book are all made from negatives which were used to produce stereographs. A stereograph consists of a pair of photographic prints which were designed to be viewed side by side to produce the effect of depth. The prints were viewed through a stereoscope, an optical device of great popularity with the Victorians. These negatives are part of the W. M. Lawrence Collection in the National Library of Ireland, although it seems they belonged originally to Lawrence's brother, J. F. Lawrence[4]. Who actually took the photographs is not known. There are some 3,000 negatives in the collection, of which 66 are of Belfast. We have selected 44, rejecting the others because of their technical inferiority or because they are very similar to views which were used in *No mean city*. Some of the photographs can be dated very precisely, but all belong to the period 1864-80.

THE TOWN

These views show Belfast at a time of great development and change. By 1861 the population of the town stood at 119, 393, compared with around 20,000 in 1800. But by 1881 the figure was

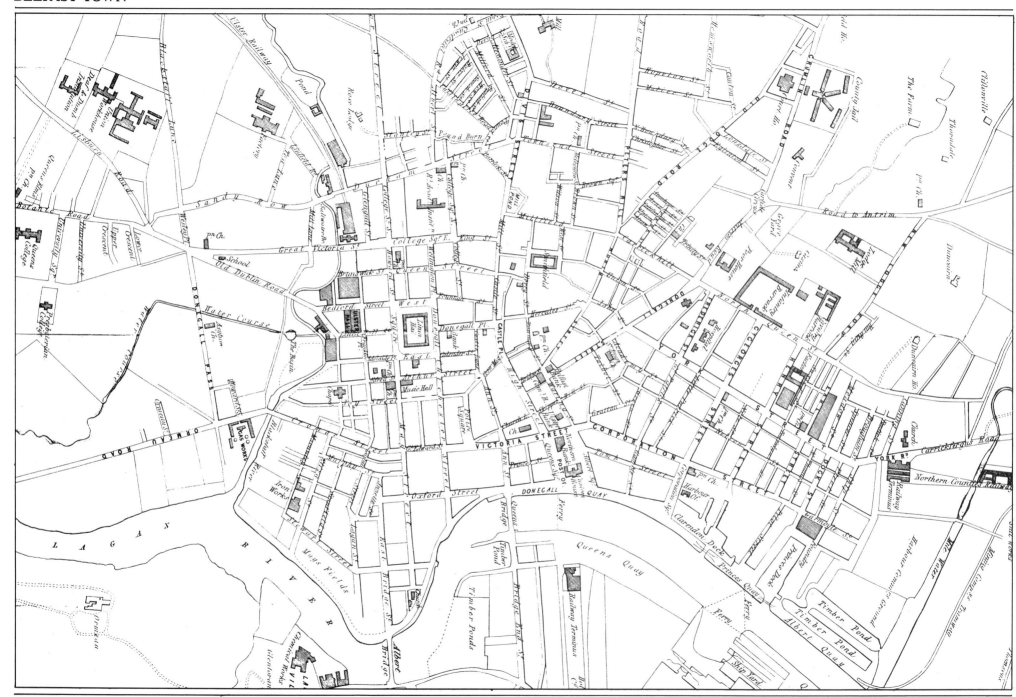

208,122 and the formal recognition of Belfast as a city followed only 7 years later[5]. The photographs give us a good picture of the town in these important decades 1860-80. The prints of the White Linen Hall and St Anne's are evidence of parts of the Georgian town which still survived at this time. Both buildings would be swept away before long and replaced with new structures, considered more fitting to a new city. As one can see, some private residences still survived in the early 1870s in Donegall Place but the street was now mostly commercial and by the mid 1880s it had become the principal shopping thoroughfare. Views of the new Elmwood and Fitzroy churches are reminders of population movement outwards to the suburbs.

At the heart of all this development was the growth in the commerce and industry of Belfast. Bedford Street with its linen warehouses, built in the 1850s and 1860s, is evidence of the town's major industry. By the early decades of the second half of the nineteenth century shipbuilding was becoming another important Belfast industry: we are reminded of this, indirectly, by the photograph of the fountain in the Crystal Palace on Queen's Island which was demolished in the 1870s to make way for the expanding shipyards. Views of the 'Bangor Boat' record what became one of the most popular excursions for the workers of Belfast in the late nineteenth and early twentieth centuries.

Right up to the middle of the nineteenth century writers on Belfast commented on the many benevolent, literary and artistic societies in the town which had given it the name of 'Athens of the north'. Pictures of the museum in College Square and the Music Hall in May Street are records of this. During the second half of the century, however, it is clear that Belfast was more renowned for its business sense than its cultural awareness. Religious tolerance also declined over the century. The opening in 1815 of the first St Patrick's Catholic Church (seen here in the 1860s) was attended by many leading protestants, but this did not happen when the second St Patrick's was consecrated in 1877. The photograph of the Model School reminds us of an experiment in non-denominational education which failed in the 1870s: on the other hand, the view of Queen's College is a reminder of one which succeeded.

The photographs also illustrate the great changes in building style which occurred in Belfast. Most of the major buildings of the eighteenth and early nineteenth centuries were the work of visiting architects. Only in the 1830s with men such as Thomas Duff, Thomas Jackson and Charles Lanyon did a local school of architects begin to emerge. The important new buildings which the expanding town required by the mid nineteenth century, such as the Custom House, Harbour Office and Town Hall, gave these architects an opportunity to show their skill. In broad design they followed general developments, moving from correct classicism to the equally serious revival of other styles: gothic for churches; Tudor for educational and institutional buildings; and vigorous Italianate for the main mercantile and public edifices of the town.

These photographs, therefore, give us an invaluable picture of Belfast in this important period. Of course, they do not cover all aspects of life in the town. There are no views of the slum dwellings, so graphically described in the 1850s by the Rev. William O'Hanlon[6]. The new industrial and suburban houses, which were being constructed in great quantity in this period, are not covered. No photographs of people at work are seen. Reflecting the taste of most contemporary photographers, our photographer contented himself with taking pictures of only the principal buildings and streets. Even these views often lack the presence of people, which can so enhance a photograph, but with the state of photographic science at the time, any movement caused a blur in the print and so photographers often preferred not to have people in their picture. Still, we must be very grateful for the excellent views which we do have.

THE TOUR

In *No mean city* we organised the material after the fashion of an Edwardian tour of the city, starting in Castle Place. This time we have returned to *c*.1870. Imagine that you have just arrived at the railway station in Great Victoria Street on your first visit to Belfast. Follow in the footsteps of William Thackeray, J. B. Doyle, William McComb and other writers of Victorian travel and guide books. Take a tour of the bustling streets and fine buildings of this 'new and improving'[7] town called Belfast.

Map of Belfast, 1861, from *McComb's guide to Belfast* . . . (Belfast, 1861)

ULSTER RAILWAY TERMINUS, GREAT VICTORIA STREET

Visitors arriving by train from the south in the 1860s would have been impressed by the railway terminus and headquarters in Great Victoria Street. Trains of the Ulster Railway Company first ran between Belfast and Lisburn in 1839. The line was then extended in stages to the west and south of the country. Completion of a permanent bridge over the Boyne in 1855 brought direct rail contact between Dublin and Belfast.

The original station on the site was built by the engineer, Thomas Jackson Woodhouse.[1] He had been the first county surveyor of Antrim but resigned in order to specialise in railway works. The second station, completed in 1848, was designed by John Godwin who came from Swansea as company engineer.[2] Later he combined his duties with those of the first professor of civil engineering at the new Queen's College. He became a close friend of Charles Lanyon, who had succeeded Woodhouse as county surveyor. It is Lanyon's distinctive brand of Italianate architecture which provided the example for Godwin's station.

In a typical early Victorian way the station is seen as a modern mercantile revival of a Renaissance Italian palazzo with heavily rusticated lower floor and more decorative and refined *piano nobile* above. The heavy cornice is the style's most recognisable feature. Passengers passed through the large portico with its couple Tuscan Doric columns to the carriages, traps and jaunting cars waiting on the cobbled forecourt.

Most of the station was demolished in 1967. All that remains is part of Woodhouse's original passenger shed. This view is the earliest known photograph of the station and is dated *c.* 1870. It shows the building before the addition of the *porte cochere* of cast iron and glass, added in 1891.[3]

FISHERWICK PLACE PRESBYTERIAN CHURCH

Across the road from the station, Fisherwick Place Presbyterian Church stood at the corner of Howard Street. The building was opened for worship on 23rd September 1827 by Dr Thomas Chalmers, perhaps the most famous Scottish preacher of his generation[1]. This church was the first in Ulster where presbyterians decided to have a full portico. This started a fashion for greater elaboration and Neo-classical precision in church building which was to last until mid-century.

The portico with its triangular pediment and four Ionic columns (with ram's horn capitals) was well integrated with the rest of the church. Others, and there were many, were less successful. During a brief visit to Belfast in 1842, William Thackeray, the famous novelist, remarked on the great number of meeting houses and stated how that they had a 'thick-set citizen look. Porticoes have they, to be sure, and ornaments Doric, Ionic, and what not; but the meeting house peeps through all these classical friezes and entablatures'[2].

The church was designed by Thomas Duff, a Newry architect who also had an office in Belfast. It was set well back from the street behind fine gates and railings. After the tide of building taste had changed from classic to gothic and members of the congregation had moved to the suburbs, the church was sold in 1898 to the General Assembly as a site for the Church House and Assembly Hall. The new Fisherwick Church was opened on the Malone Road in April 1901[3].

STATUES OF THE EARL OF BELFAST AND THE REV. HENRY COOKE, COLLEGE SQUARE EAST

Beyond Fisherwick Place the visitor would have come to College Square, so-called because it was built around the Royal Belfast Academical Institution, generally called 'Inst', which originally provided both grammar and university level education. Founded in 1810, its main structure was completed in 1814 to designs by Sir John Soane. The building with its giant coupled pilasters is visible in the background of both these photographs.

Like Inst, the statue at its gates of Frederick Richard, Earl of Belfast (1827-53), was paid for by public subscription. Erected in 1855 it was the town's first public statue. Lord Belfast was a son of the third Marquis of Donegall. A poet and composer, he died at an early age in Naples. His statue by Patrick McDowell (1790-1870) was of bronze but was eventually

painted black which caused him to be known as the 'black man'! The photograph on the left, the only one known of the statue in its original position shows that it was not originally painted black and that it did not face Inst, as is sometimes believed, but looked towards Wellington Place.

As if Belfast could not sustain the display of two public statues, it was decided in 1876 that Lord Belfast should be removed (first to the town hall, then to the public library and finally to its present home in the city hall) and be replaced by a figure of the Rev. Henry Cooke. This leader of mid-Victorian presbyterian orthodoxy was a prominent opponent of the more liberal attitudes propounded at Inst to which he turns his back. The statue in bronze was by Samuel Ferres Lynn (1834-1876), a brother of the distinguished Belfast architect W. H. Lynn, and a former student of Patrick McDowell. It was inaugurated at a great Orange occasion in April 1876.

THE MUSEUM, COLLEGE SQUARE NORTH

In the middle of the north side of College Square, enjoying the southern prospect across the cricket lawns of 'Inst', was the Museum of the Belfast Natural History and Philosophical Society. The society was founded in 1821 by a group of youthful enthusiasts with a common interest in studying natural history, especially of Ireland. After less than a decade, the society decided to build its own premises where members could meet, conduct experiments and gather specimens in a scientific way to be displayed for public education and enjoyment. The resulting museum was the first in Ireland to be erected by voluntary subscriptions. Its foundation stone was laid in May 1830[1].

The building, designed by Thomas Duff of Newry and his young Belfast partner, Thomas Jackson, was intended as an architectural embodiment of the enlightened and democratic attitudes to which it owed its origins. Inevitably the Greek revival style was employed and almost equally inevitably the architects looked to the most recently published volume of *The antiquities of Athens* for inspiration. The most obvious quotation from the antique in a facade full of classical pieces is the use of a very correct portico from the Tower of the Winds, Athens[2].

As the museum's collections expanded so did the number of visitors. Eventually the need for special curatorial care and professional management became clear and in 1910 it was decided to present the collections to the Belfast Municipal Museum; the transfer was delayed until the new building was completed in 1929[3].

College Square remained residential throughout the nineteenth century, and until after the Great War. Occupied originally by prosperous merchants, industrialists and academics connected with Inst, it became favoured by surgeons and medical specialists. The block of two houses to the right of the museum in the photograph were occupied in 1861 by Alexander Hawkins, proprietor of the Bank Buildings, and Robert Patterson who had a hardware business and was also a founder member of the B.N.H.P.S.. Eventually the two houses were united as the Deaf and Dumb Institute. The house on the other side of the museum was occupied at the end of the century by William Whitla, Professor of Materia Medica at the Queen's College[4].

The character of all the buildings on the north side of the square, and indeed of the square itself, was totally ruined by the erection of the Municipal Technical Institute (completed 1905).

CHRIST CHURCH (CHURCH OF IRELAND), COLLEGE SQUARE NORTH

Proceeding westward beyond the museum along College Square, the visitor would have come to Christ Church (Church of Ireland), completed in 1833 for the celebrated (or, according to taste, notorious) Rev. Dr Thomas Drew, whose preaching was supposed to have prompted every response from meek reason to malicious riot. The church held 1,600 and was frequently full. As part of a campaign to stop idleness, drunkenness and impropriety during holidays Dr Drew conducted excursions with groups of boys and girls walking behind banners from the town centre to Stranmillis and Belvoir with sermons before and after the event[1]

The church may also be regarded as solid, sober and proper in its architecture. Although to Victorians it was 'plain and unassuming'[2] it is a fine example of late-Georgian Neo-classicism. It is also an example of Thackeray's observation that buildings and facades in Belfast seemed not to match each other. Here at least the side windows are set in recessed arches and linked by a string course. Nevertheless the brick of the wall is in great contrast to the cut-stone sophistication of the main front with its two giant Ionic columns set as a recessed portico to flank the central doorway. Inside the layout followed the long established convention with U-shaped gallery and focal pulpit. Only a few Victorian alterations, such as moving the pulpit from the main access to give prominence to the holy table, distinguish it from contemporary meeting houses.

Its architect was William Farrell of Dublin[3] a designer of distinguished courthouses (Cavan, Enniskillen) and mansions (Colebrooke, Cecil Manor) in the Neo-classical style, and of spikey gothic churches (Enniskillen, Monaghan, Armagh). In Belfast, however, no protestant church had hitherto used the gothic style, so Farrell designed a church which might pass as a court house. Ten years later the presbyterians built a gothic church, immediately opposite Christ Church. That church was closed in 1963 and demolished three years later. Christ Church remains.

BEDFORD STREET FROM DONEGALL SQUARE

Bedford Street, back nearer the town centre, was laid out in the 1850s on the previously unpromising but then newly drained land to the south of Donegall Square. It was a straight projection of the west side of the square southwards as far as the line of the old Dublin Road where it crossed the Blackstaff River. It was never a residential street but, on the contrary, was lined from the outset with three- and four-storey warehouses. These were straightforward working buildings with large floor areas lit by regularly spaced windows. The functional interiors did not, however, prevent many of these buildings having quite distinguished facades, with the repeated windows, sometimes linked by simple decoration, giving a unifying rhythm and strength.

The building on the left of the photograph below the tree was originally occupied by several linen manufacturers and merchants. It was later replaced by the Scottish Temperance Life Assurance Buildings, completed in 1904[1]

On the right the nearest block was occupied in the 1860s by Messrs Robert and John Workman who manufactured 'fair linen' and sewed muslin items. Other firms shared the premises, notably James Kennedy, the 'power-loom cotton and muslin manufacturer' who occupied the far end of the block. Mr Kennedy did not have to travel far to work because he lived in Donegall Square West[2]

The slightly taller block beyond this, incorporating nos 9-15, was one of the earliest buildings in the street, being described as recently completed in 1852[3] Eventually this block and the one beyond, built in 1869[4] were taken over by William Ewart and Sons, the enormously successful linen manufacturers.

THE ULSTER HALL, BEDFORD STREET

Half way along Bedford Street on its east side there was the only building in the thoroughfare not devoted to industry or commerce. The Ulster Hall was projected by a joint-stock company (so after all it, too, was intended to make money) which held a competition for its design in 1860. This was won by W. J. Barre,[1] a young Newry architect, who promptly moved to Belfast in order to supervise the works; this was not just a matter of convenience but also of necessity for there had been attempts by more established, jealous members of the Belfast architectural profession to have Barre relieved of the responsibility of supervising the works because of his inexperience. Everyone was worried about the stability of the building; no-one was impolite enough to mention the large fees which would go to the supervising architect. But Barre was not supplanted, and the hall, considered by the generation that saw its building as 'one of the largest and most splendid public edifices in Belfast',[2] was opened in 1862.

This must be one of the earliest photographs of the hall. It was taken even before its neighbour, a warehouse, also designed by Barre (who died in 1867), had been built.[3] Although most of the decoration was in the great auditorium, the main facade was also quite impressive in a dignified way which suited Belfast. It was set back from the line of the street; this gave it some importance and also allowed a projecting *porte-cochere* or portico into which carriages could pass.

THE QUEEN'S COLLEGE, UNIVERSITY ROAD

Three quarters of a mile southwards from Bedford Steeet along the Old Dublin Road and Botanic Road (as early Victorians called University Road) the visitor would have come to The Queen's College, founded by parliamentary act in 1845 and opened for students a few weeks after its inspection in August 1849 by Queen Victoria and Prince Albert. It was one of three Queen's Colleges set up in Ireland to provide non-denominational, higher education[1].

'The situation of the building', wrote Doyle a few years later, 'is well chosen. It is sufficiently removed from the bustle of the town, and not too far for the convenience of the students resident in Belfast. This very beautiful building . . . is in the Tudor style, built with bright red brick, and profusely ornamented with cut stone . . . A massive tower, about eighty feet in height, rises over the principal entrance . . . the internal arrangements are commodious and elegant, and although to an eye accustomed to the venerable and time-worn halls of Trinity or of Oxford and Cambridge, they have somewhat of a raw and unpoetical effect, yet it cannot be denied that they are well adapted to the great purposes for which they were designed'[2].

The other advantage of the situation was that the college had as its neighbour the Botanic Gardens, begun on their present site in 1829. Together college and gardens provided a magnet for Belfast's mid-Victorian south-westerly expansion. After some initial problems the college had succeeded by the early twentieth century in gaining the support of the whole community. Queen's became a university in its own right in 1908.

ELMWOOD PRESBYTERIAN CHURCH, UNIVERSITY ROAD

Elmwood Presbyterian Church, across the road from Queen's, was one of Belfast's most individual churches. Unlike many suburban congregations it did not have its origins in a town centre foundation but was simply the result of a meeting of a few friends who were invited to tea by Robert Workman of Windsor on 5th November 1858. Services were originally held in a classroom of the Assembly's College, but then a site was offered by Robert Corry: his son, John, who although working in the London Office of the family firm also planned buildings occasionally, supplied the design[1].

Elmwood Church, built 1860-2, is a typical High Victorian mixture of historic styles with Italian origins dominating. The tower manages to have a spire on top of a campanile and achieves the character of a pagoda. Although part of the original design, the tower was not completed until 1872[2].

The houses on the left were called University Terrace because of their proximity to the new college. They were built before the church in the early 1850s and they then lined up along the original lane down to the Lisburn Road. Soon after, the new alignment, Elmwood Avenue, was chosen on the near side of the church. Between houses and church there is a glimpse of the roof of Methodist College, built 1865-8. The gateway on the right led to the original Queen's Elms, a terrace in the 'Jacobethan' style built opposite to Queen's College in 1859[3].

DEAF AND DUMB INSTITUTE FROM ELMWOOD AVENUE
(ORIGINALLY GREGG'S LANE)

As this photograph vividly shows, direct access from Queen's to the Lisburn Road in the mid-Victorian period was not by a wide thoroughfare but by a rough track. Running across land owned by Cranston Gregg, whose house Elmwood stood just to its north, it was known simply as Gregg's Lane. The formal line of Elmwood Avenue was laid out soon after the Presbyterian church had been built with a manse (of 1866) blocking the old lane on its south side. Houses were built along the south side of the avenue between 1868 and 1886, starting at the Queen's end[1].

On the north side, the gardens around Elmwood remained intact until the end of the century. All Souls Non-subscribing Presbyterian Church, successor of the original second Belfast Congregation in Rosemary Street, was built near the Lisburn Road end in 1895; the intervening space was gradually filled with university buildings from the 1920s. During all this development the focus at the west end, across the Lisburn Road, was the Deaf and Dumb Institute.

DEAF AND DUMB INSTITUTE, LISBURN ROAD

The Institute for the Deaf and Dumb and Blind had been founded in a back room of the Congregational Church in Donegall Street in 1831. It expanded rapidly, moved three times in the next decade, and arrived finally at a five acre site off the Lisburn Road. The new building was begun in 1843 and declared open on 24th September 1845. Cranston Gregg of Elmwood was the contractor: it cost £11,500[1]. Charles Lanyon's design was based on Elizabethan almshouses, a suitable historical style to associate with the new purpose.

The institute's object was to afford to afflicted children a religious and literary education, and also to teach them useful trades. 'The pupils have progressed in the most satisfactory manner', wrote Doyle almost a decade after the opening of the new building, 'and nothing is more calculated to awaken feelings of thankfulness, than a visit to a place where science and art have triumphed over apparently insuperable natural defects, and where, if the lost senses be not restored, their loss is compensated for in a manner that renders the burden of the privation comparatively light'[2].

FITZROY AVENUE PRESBYTERIAN CHURCH

The church may seem oddly named because it is at the corner of University Street and Rugby Road, and Fitzroy is merely a minor adjacent street. The reason for this is that when the site was bought in 1872 for the congregation, originally from Alfred Street Presbyterian Church, University Street ran only from University Road to Botanic Avenue: from this point onwards the street was called Fitzroy Avenue and its name was changed to University Street only in the mid 1870s. The church was one of a number rebuilt by congregations which had formerly been based in the town centre but now found that members had migrated to the new residential areas which were being built to house the growing population.[1]

Plans for the Church were drawn up by Robert Magill Young of the local firm of Young and Mackenzie.[2] His scheme with tower linked to church only by a bridge which gives access to the gallery, clearly derives from Sinclair Seamen's Church (see p.38).

ALFRED STREET PRESBYTERIAN CHURCH

Opened in 1837, the church replaced an earlier building of 1822 in Alfred Place which was then taken over by two other congregations who eventually set up their own churches elsewhere[1]. The first minister of both the original and the new Alfred Street church was the celebrated Rev. Dr John Edgar, a leading temperance reformer. He began his drive for temperance in 1829 when he opened his parlour window and 'poured out before his house in Alfred Street the remaining part of a gallon of old malt whiskey purchased some time before for family consumption'[2]. The building on the right of the church in the photograph is the manse where this act took place.

In 1872 the church was sold and the congregation worshipped in Clarence Place Hall before moving to their new meeting house in Fitzroy Avenue. The old church was drastically altered and used for commercial purposes before being demolished. This photograph can be dated *c.* 1864 because of the Belfast Indemnity Bill poster on the wall to the left of the church. The bill was passed in 1864 and marked the settlement in a long dispute between some Belfast citizens and the town council over misuse of rates' money.

ST MALACHY'S CATHOLIC CHURCH

The dedication in 1844 of the third Roman Catholic church in Belfast to St Malachy, the great organiser of the Irish medieval church, was as inevitable as that of the first to St Mary (1784) and of the second to St Patrick (1815). Although it never achieved the distinction, it was clearly intended to serve as and look like a cathedral. Unlike the earlier churches it was not tucked away on a restricted site but had a spacious setting on part of McClean's Field to the west of Joy Street which was just being built. Further west, the direction from which this photograph was taken, the open Chapel Fields stretched southwards to the banks of the Blackstaff. They remained free of building until Alfred Street was extended southwards, a quarter of a century later.

From the designs of 14 competitors, those of Thomas Jackson were selected in 1841[1]. Evidently the collegiate Tudor gothic style used so successfully by his former senior partner, Thomas Duff, at Newry, Dundalk and Armagh, appealed to the judges[2]. By this time the serious revival of gothic forms was regarded not so much as a fashion as a duty in catholic church building. The generous bequest of Captain Thomas Griffith made decorative elaboration possible. Jackson was skilful enough to extend a fairly conventional, rectangular, galleried hall into a cruciform layout with Tudor windows, battlements, buttresses, finials and chess-rook turrets outside, and a pendant vaulted triumph within.

As this very early photograph shows, the church originally had no main bell tower, but a bell was hung in the left of the two front turrets. This bell, hung in 1842, was damaged in 1845, possibly because its mounting in the turret was unstable. A new bell, the largest in Belfast, was later mounted in a central tower with spire which was blessed in 1868. The central tower was itself subsequently rebuilt without a spire.

MAY STREET PRESBYTERIAN CHURCH

On the corner opposite Alfred Street Church the visitor would have seen May Street Presbyterian Church, built in 1828-9 to designs by William Smith for the celebrated Rev. Dr Henry Cooke.[1] Doyle, betraying a typical Victorian disregard for Neo-classicism, no matter how good, thought the church was 'rendered more attractive by the well-known eloquence of the preacher, rather than by its architectural pretensions'.[2] McComb on the contrary referred to it as a 'fine structure', remarked on its 'beautiful pediment' and stated that 'the style of ornamentation in the interior is much admired'.[3] Sittings of the General Assembly, when it met in Belfast, were usually held in the church.

Beside the church was the school house, with its Roman Doric columns and urns on the parapets, designed by John Boyd (1858-9).[4] The tall terrace of five houses beyond the school was called Clarendon Place and built *c*.1850.[5] It was for a time considered rather a grand place to live. Three merchants and a 'gentleman' were resident in 1852, and several surgeons moved in before the end of the century. Gradually, however, the houses became unmanageably large and equally important, unfashionably placed. They became offices and small manufactories for handkerchiefs and stained glass. They were demolished in 1926.

MUSIC HALL, MAY STREET

Immediately opposite May Street Presbyterian Church stood the Music Hall. It was built for the Anacreontic Society,[1] which was named after an Ionian Greek music teacher and lyric poet of the sixth century, B.C., who wrote hymns and love songs which were remarkable for their combination of fancy and wit. His language was said to be an Ionic vernacular, and it is (perhaps accidentally) appropriate that the Music Hall adopts the Ionic style of architecture.

Thomas Jackson's designs for the hall were among his, and Belfast's, most polished Neo-classical designs, presenting sophisticated facades to both May Street and Upper Arthur Street.[2] The main hall had a full orchestral stage, a gallery over the entrance hall and staircase, and plaster roundels with putti symbolising the elements. The hall was opened with a grand concert in 1839.

Seasons of concerts were held annually. A typical programme on Thursday, 28th December, 1842, included music by Haydn, overtures by Auber and Bernhard Romberg, glees and choruses, and a violincello obligato by a Mr Lidel, whose 'command over that rather ungainly instrument is surprising'.[3]

Audiences, however, were not always large in an auditorium which could seat 800. Various attempts, including the opening of wax works, were made to boost attendance. The minor hall and basements were let to outside organisations such as Church Lads, and the Y.M.C.A. gymnasium was in one part of the building during the Edwardian period, under the watchful eye of an ex-sergeant Gilbert. After a spell as a church, very sadly the building was demolished in 1983.

DONEGALL SQUARE METHODIST CHURCH, DONEGALL SQUARE EAST

Just around the corner from May Street was Donegall Square Methodist Church, imposingly sited at the centre of the east side of the Square with terraced Georgian houses on each side. The original Methodist square church in Belfast had been built in 1786 in Fountain Street. In 1806, when the first houses were being built around the White Linen Hall to form Donegall Square, the Methodists chose the prestigious site in the middle of the east side for a new church. As the town grew this church proved too small and was rebuilt to designs by Isaac Farrell of Dublin with a full-scale, six column Corinthian portico supporting a great triangular pediment.[1] This was to be one of the last classical temples in this 'Athens of the north'; even as it was being built, the tide of taste and of philosophy was drawing church designers towards the gothic revival.

The foundation stone was laid in July 1846 and the church opened on 20th June 1847. It was designed to accommodate 1,500 for worship, and the church was raised up to allow a schoolroom in the basement which could seat 1,000 children. The church was by the outstanding builder of the day, James Carlisle, whose name is remembered in the great church at Carlisle Circus, built thirty years later.

In 1849 an organ was installed and so was the much-travelled organist John Willis, formerly of St Anne's Church in Donegall Street. Prior to this, according to the church history, Willis 'had held a similar position in connection with St Patrick's Roman Catholic Church in the same street, where his services were dispensed with because he played the popular Orange air 'The Boyne Water' at a service, probably the only occasion on which this was ever played in an Irish Roman Catholic Church'. He had less time to be controversial in Donegall Square. The church had not been long opened when it was accidentally destroyed by fire. Works were again swift as in the previous church. The fire was in September 1849 but the church opened in 1850.

The photograph gives a vivid idea of the character of Donegall Square when it was still largely a residential area near the southern edge of the town. 'The houses', wrote Thackeray in 1843, 'are as handsome as, at Dublin, with this advantage, that the people seem to live in them'.[2]

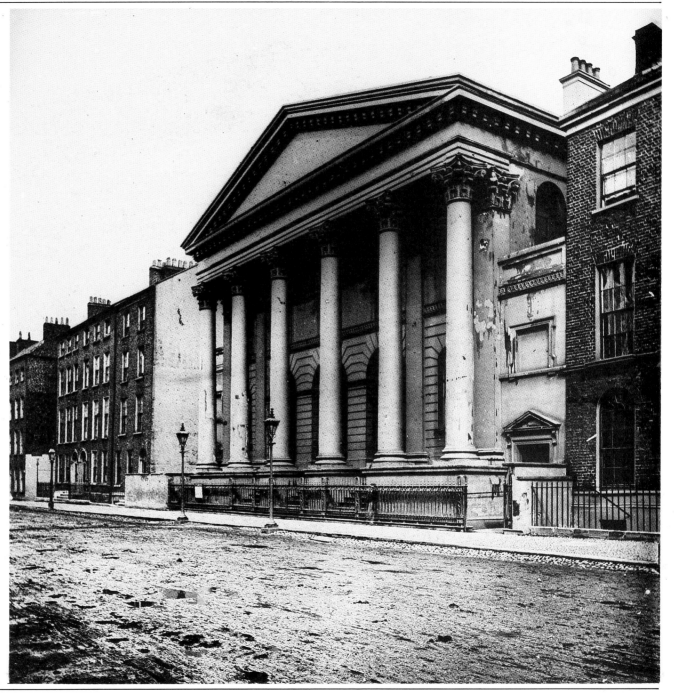

DONEGALL SQUARE, WHITE LINEN HALL

Looking out from the portico of the Methodist Church a mid-Victorian visitor would have seen the east range of the White Linen Hall 'an extensive quadrangular building occupying the centre of Donegall Square. It was erected in 1785 in consequence of the inconvenience which the linen trade of Belfast experienced from the transaction theretofore of the business of that branch of the trade at so great a distance as Dublin, where the agents concerned . . . chiefly resided . . . Belfast is acknowledged as the chief point of export for the entire of the linen districts'[1]. Lord Donegall gave the ground, and, as so often in Georgian Belfast, enterprise took over. Subscriptions were collected towards the cost of building and £17,550 was quickly subscribed, not only by linen merchants but by others who, though not directly involved with the trade, were keen to support a venture which would promote the prosperity of the whole Belfast community. The building appears to have been designed by Roger Mulholland[2].

The quadrangle of buildings consisted largely of rather utilitarian two-storey offices and stores. The main block in the centre of the north side was taller and more elaborate with 'rusticated' window surrounds and surmounting tower with a clock below a cupola. This block provided the visual focus for Donegall Place then known as Linen Hall Street. Through the archway are seen houses in Castle Place at the far end of the street. The building was also an intellectual focus. 'Under the clock tower . . . is the Belfast Library, the property of the Belfast Society for promoting knowledge, founded in 1788. The library which contains about 20,000 volumes, besides maps, charts and other appliances is one of the best selected in the Kingdom, being especially rich in the departments of history, biography, books of reference, and works relating to Ireland. The books are admirably classified whilst the reading room, which is airy and spacious contains on its tables almost every periodical of note'[3]. The Linen Hall library moved to its present home when the Linen Hall itself was demolished in 1898 to make way for the City Hall. Nevertheless, the building achieved a kind of immortality both in its name, which the library retains, and as the centrepiece of the library's bookplate.

DONEGALL PLACE AND THE ROYAL HOTEL

This was the view from the windows of the Linen Hall Library. It extended the length of Donegall Place to the houses on the north side of Castle Place, before the opening of Royal Avenue in the 1880s. The street, laid out as part of Lord Donegall's improvements and built during the 1780s and 1790s, became the most desirable residential thoroughfare in town and only in the mid-19th century did its character begin to change towards business and shopping.[1] The photograph gives a good idea of the street's appearance as this change took place. On the right two Georgian houses look small beside the Bank of Ireland, a recent arrival in 1858-9, just beyond. Further along shops have appeared on both sides.

On the left the town house of Lord Donegall for fifty years became the Royal Hotel under the management of Charles Kerns, a former butler to the Donegall family. It had many famous visitors including the Royal Dukes of Connaught and Clarence, Daniel O'Connell, Jenny Lind 'The Swedish Nightingale', John Bright, Mr and Mrs Charles Kean, and Lord John Russell.[2] Thackeray thought it 'as comfortable and well-ordered an establishment as the most fastidious can desire, and with an advantage . . . that dinners which cost seven shillings at London taverns are here served for half-a-crown . . . here the wine is good, whereas the port-wine in England is not port . . .'[3]

The proprietors guarded its distinctive character carefully. In 1891 it was reported that 'It still preserves its ancient reputation as a high-class establishment, catering for the nobility and gentry who patronise it, and distinguished from other establishments which seek their customers among the commercial classes. In fact no commercial accommodation is afforded here . . .'[4] By 1898 it had closed, perhaps because of this failure to move with the times, and was replaced by shops and offices.

CASTLE PLACE

While Donegall Place still remained partly residential in the mid nineteenth century, Castle Place round the corner had become very commercial. The Georgian houses had, for the most part, been pulled down in groups and rebuilt on a grander scale, and with more attention to facade decoration as Victorians liked. On the right at the corner of Donegall Place was Castle Buildings occupying part of the site of Belfast's original castle which was built early in the seventeenth century for Sir Arthur Chichester, and destroyed by fire in 1708. For very many years it was known as Gibson's Corner because of the shop which can be seen in the photograph which was owned by William Gibson of Phoenix Lodge, Dunmurry, who was 'watchmaker, jeweller, silversmith, optician, and manufacturer of bog oak jewellery'[1].

This view is of particular interest because of the variety of horse-drawn traffic. Note the double decker horse tram which replaced the single decker vehicle in 1878 (see p.2 and p.31). Beyond Castle Place can be seen High Street, the heart of the seventeenth century town which owes its irregular line to the course of the Farsett River along which it is built. The river still runs in culverts below Castle Place and High Street.

Until the 1870s the business centre of Belfast lay in Donegall Street, Waring Street, Rosemary Street and Bridge Street. But this changed with the introduction of the trams which had their terminus in Castle Place, or Castle Junction as it was now called. The centre moved to Castle Place and Donegall Place, a development which was strengthened by the opening of Royal Avenue in the first half of the 1880s.

THEATRE ROYAL, ARTHUR SQUARE

The second Theatre Royal in Arthur Square, as seen in this rare photograph, was opened in 1871[1]. The person responsible for launching this new undertaking was J. F. Warden who combined the jobs of theatre manager and actor. He had run the original Theatre Royal (built 1793) for a time but by the late 1860s he believed that the fast-growing Belfast population needed a grand, large, new theatre. His instinct proved correct and the theatre was extremely successful. By the 1870s travelling companies had become the mainstay of the provincial theatrical world and Belfast citizens had the opportunity to see many of the best companies of actors and singers. The Theatre Royal was badly damaged by fire in 1881 but it was soon rebuilt although without the surmounting pediment and its royal arms[2].

The architect of the second Theatre Royal was Charles Sherry. He died, however, before the theatre was completed and the remaining work was supervised by Charles Lanyon's firm[3]. Medallions on the walls epicted famous writers and actors. These were the work of Thomas Fitzpatrick who was also responsible for the carvings on the Ulster Bank and the Custom House.

THE TOWN HALL, VICTORIA STREET

Access eastwards towards the river from Arthur Square in the early nineteenth century was either by Ann Street, or by a slight southward detour along William Street South and through Police Square, so-named from the town constabulary offices which once stood at its western end. Its previous name was Poultry Square, presumably because it was the site of the hen market. It stood at the head of a dock reaching in from the Lagan. Only later in Victoria's reign was it named after her, and thus associated with Victoria Street which was a mid-century improvement, linking the foot of High Street (marked here by the Albert Clock in the distance) and the markets at the river end of Chichester Street.[1]

Police Square is the gap on the left marked by the Jaffe Memorial Fountain (see right photograph also) beyond which Upper Church Lane leaves Victoria Street at an angle. The prow-shaped building on the corner was built for John Trueman, baker and flour merchant, and 'nearly complete' in February 1868.[2]

On the right (see left photograph also) is the Town Hall and Municipal Buildings for which the design was selected in competition in Janary 1869, the winner being Anthony Jackson.[3] The design, a sturdy brick essay in mixed historical styles was not universally admired; some thought it insufficiently imposing, while others, notably rival designers, advocated the use of classicism for important civic buildings such as this. Their day was to come when this building was superceded by the City Hall in 1906. The design was extended in execution to include a new police barracks and the fire alarm bell.

The gap beyond the Town Hall was to have been the site of the Central Railway Station which would have provided a link between the other main stations in York Street, Great Victoria Street and over the river on Queen's Quay. Although the track was laid and the river bridge built, a small train station on the Laganbank Road was all that seemed necessary and no great terminus was built beside the Town Hall. Meanwhile it was used as a temporary depot for slate, tile fire clay and bricks, and later for a group of fruiterers' stalls, until permanent buildings were erected at the end of the century. The tram in the street is one of the single decker variety which was phased out after 1878.

The Jaffe Fountain set up in 1874 was a memorial to Daniel Joseph Jaffe, a linen merchant originally from Hamburg who built Belfast's first synagogue, and was father of a Lord Mayor, Sir Otto Jaffe.

The left hand view of the Town Hall was taken from beside the Jaffe Fountain at the east end of Police Square, looking south-eastwards. In the distance behind the fountain are the houses of Great Edward Street, later absorbed as part of Victoria Street, which joined Chichester Street to May Street. The splendid array of flags on the Town Hall suggests that this was a special occasion.

NORTHERN BANK, VICTORIA STREET

The Northern Banking Company was Belfast's first joint-stock bank. It was founded in 1824. For many years it occupied the site of the present Bank Buildings in Castle Place. In mid-century, however, the commercial and trading centre-of-gravity of the town seemed to be moving towards the river. The directors then decided to devote £14,000 of their assets to providing a new head office on a prominent site at the junction of Victoria Street and Queen's Square, both named after the recent royal visit in 1849. The building was 'rapidly approaching completion' in October 1851, and was opened for business the following summer.[1]

Charles Lanyon's design was not a repetition of his own highly admired Florentine palazzo Belfast Bank, but, looking to the example of Sir John Soane's Bank of England in London, it was a vigorous exercise in neo-classical forms with a central triumphal entrance and window openings which emphasize the thickness of the rusticated walls. Giant Tuscan Doric columns support a huge entablature and cornice. Altogether it was intended as a place in which customers could feel their savings to be safe indeed. The elevated main storey was lit from clerestorey windows hidden behind the parapet;[2] this led to some criticism: 'This edifice . . . is elaborate in its architectural details; but want of elevation in keeping with its position detracts from the imposing effect which a more lofty building, on a similar plan would have presented'.[3] The posters show this photograph to have been taken in 1864.

ULSTER BANK, WARING STREET

With both the Belfast Bank and the Northern Bank comfortably housed in their new head offices, the Ulster Bank soon felt the need to demonstrate its stability and confidence in architecture.

A site was chosen midway between the other two banks half way along Waring Street. Such strategic advantage as this might have had, must have been outweighed by the narrowness of the street which made it (still makes it) quite difficult to appreciate the building. The town was, nevertheless, impressed by the newcomer. 'This is' said McComb, 'beyond question the most splendid of all the commercial buildings in Belfast; and, indeed, in architectural beauty, is second to no edifice of the kind in the country. The facade elicits the unqualified admiration of all who inspect it'[1]

The reasons for this exaggerated reaction are clear. Belfast was not used to ostentatious building, and the Ulster Bank was intended to impress. The design, chosen in competition in 1857, was by James Hamilton who worked in Glasgow where good carving stone and skilled masons were in plentiful supply. He was able to produce a florid Roman renaissance design, knowing that suitable stone could be shipped from the Clyde. Local architects, accepting the limitations of local stone, could not be so sculpturally adventurous; a measure of jealousy was perhaps inevitable and lasted some time. The bank opened in 1860. Seven years later Robert Grimshaw, then in his eighties, a founder director of the bank, died by falling down the front flight of steps, which, 'had utility been properly consulted, he would never have been required to ascend'[2]

The photograph shows the building less than ten years old but with its stone already begrimed by town smoke. It had not after all been necessary to find a Scots mason; a Belfast man, Thomas Fitzpatrick,[3] who had recently completed the sculpture on the Custom House, did all the carving on the facade including the central figure of Britannia, justice and commerce and the parapet wine jars (liquid assets?).

The late Georgian shop, on the right, was removed in 1869 and rebuilt as an extension to the Bank along Skipper Street; this time local architects, Thomas Jackson and Son, made the designs[4]

ST ANNE'S CHURCH OF IRELAND CHURCH, DONEGALL STREET FROM CHURCH STREET

J. Huband Smith evidently had this view in mind when he wrote in 1853: 'St Anne's Church, Donegall Street, being the Parish Church of Belfast, now claims our attention. It is a large and handsome building, and occupies an advantageously conspicuous situation. It is insulated from the surrounding houses, and stands back at some distance from the street. Its front is seen to most advantage from Church Street, which it faces. It was built at the expense of the first Marquis of Donegall, the foundation stone having been laid in the year 1777'[1]

The original portico was much lower reaching up only as far as the window sills above the side doors. This was not considered grand enough for the 'Athens of the north', and the full Corinthian temple front was a late Georgian improvement. This then obscured the clock which was removed from its original circular opening, and placed rather awkwardly across the belfry opening above.

Even more remarkable was the tower. 'The want of steeples has been often noticed' said Mr and Mrs Hall in 1843[2] and in 1861 McComb explained that the church was 'chiefly remarkable for its tower and handsome cupola, which are the highest stuctures of the kind in Belfast. The alluvial nature of the situation which the town occupies does not permit the erection of very lofty or weighty piles of buildings, unless the foundations are piled'[3]

The photograph gives an excellent impression of the character of side streets in the late-Georgian town, with narrow houses, built of brick and rendered, and classical shop fronts with cornices projecting over the name boards. Equally classical but less easily explained is the small female figure on a wall bracket above the doorway at the corner of Long Lane on the extreme right.

ST PATRICK'S CATHOLIC CHURCH, DONEGALL STREET

Farther along Donegall Street, past the junction with York Street, and, like St Anne's set back from the road behind railings, was the old St Patrick's Catholic Church. This was built between 1810 and 1815 to relieve the pressure on accommodation at St Mary's in Chapel Lane. Like St Mary's it was supported by contributions from all sections of the community, including, rather improbably, Lord Castlereagh who handed a hundred guineas out of his carriage to Father Hugh O'Donnell, the parish priest. who, unable to get an interview, waited for him on the Long Bridge which he had to cross to get from Belfast to his home at Mount Stewart. Prominent local protestants attended the consecration service for the new church on 3rd March 1815[1].

Perhaps because of the communal effort, and certainly because the church was more prominently placed than St Mary's, the building's progress received much publicity, both critical and supportive. Thackeray, used to more sophisticated Gothic design, thought it 'an exceedingly unprepossessing building of the Strawberry Hill or Castle of Otranto Gothic'[2].

What he did not bother to notice, and what clearly ran contrary to the more conservative architectural attitudes in the town, was that this was the first Belfast building to go completely for the gothic style. It had pointed openings, moulded decorations round the entrance door, embryonic angle buttresses rising to pointed finials, battlements on the parapets and even a gable cross. The contrary opinion, welcoming the gothic, was that 'in the eye of every scientific man it will rank high among the most elegant structures for public worship . . . and will remain a striking monument of the taste and liberality of the enlightened town in which it stands'. And so it did until it was swept away on a tide of much more serious gothic revival two generations later. The new St Patrick's was consecrated on 12 August 1877 at an impressive service, although without the ecumenical spirit which was present in 1815[3].

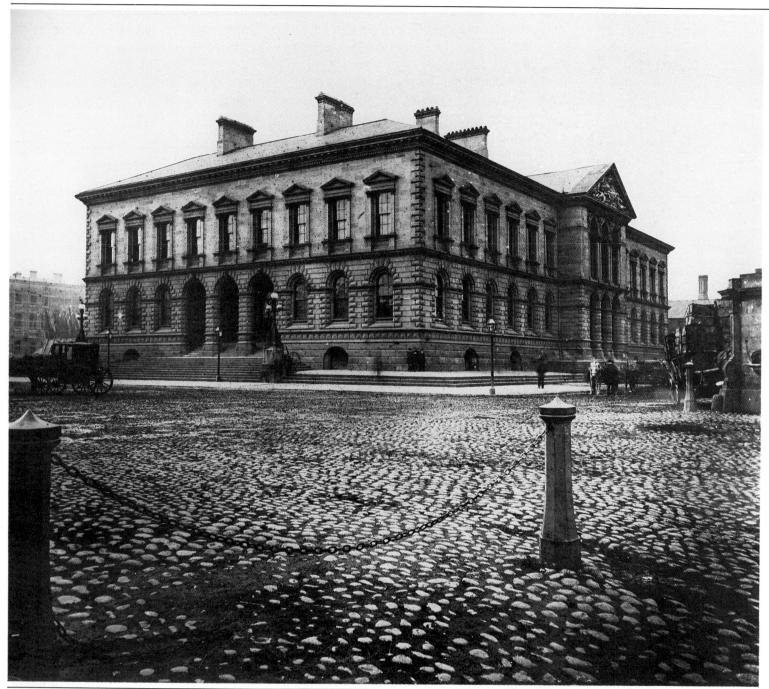

CUSTOM HOUSE

By the middle of the century new public buildings were needed in Belfast. With the completion of the new county court house and gaol on the Crumlin Road, Belfast superceded Carrickfergus as the county town of Antrim. The Custom House was planned as early as 1846 but not completed until 1857! It stands on land reclaimed from the muddy edges of the Lagan and consolidated as Donegall Quay. It was here at the foot of High street that Queen Victoria and Prince Albert came ashore for their visit in 1849. Only as recently as 1846 had the docks at the foot of High Street and Waring Street been filled; they were promptly named Queen's Square and Albert Square respectively. The Custom House stands between them.

'This pile of buildings' . . . declared McComb's 1861 guide, 'has superceded several government offices, scattered in various parts of the town,—all of which were inadequate to their purposes. The former Custom House was a disgrace to so important a seaport as Belfast. The present occupies the site of portions of two docks, the old Harbour Office, and a block of private buildings. It has four fronts, the principal one of which faces the river . . . the cost exceeded £30,000. Not only the Customs' business of the port, but also that of the Post-Office, Income Tax and Stamp Offices, Inland Revenue and Government Emigration departments etc., is transacted here'[2]

Because of the many different departments it contained, the building had several entrances, and, as these photographs show, these have changed over the years. There was a main Customs entrance beneath the central pediment on the river front facing east. The Stamp Office was in the north wing. In the middle of the south elevation was the triple-arched entrance to the Post Office, visible in two views here. The third view shows that this was later blocked and a new entrance with double stairs was made at the west end of the south wing. This, too, was later removed, possibly when the new G.P.O. was opened in Royal Avenue in 1886[3]. There were also several entrance doors around the open court on the west.

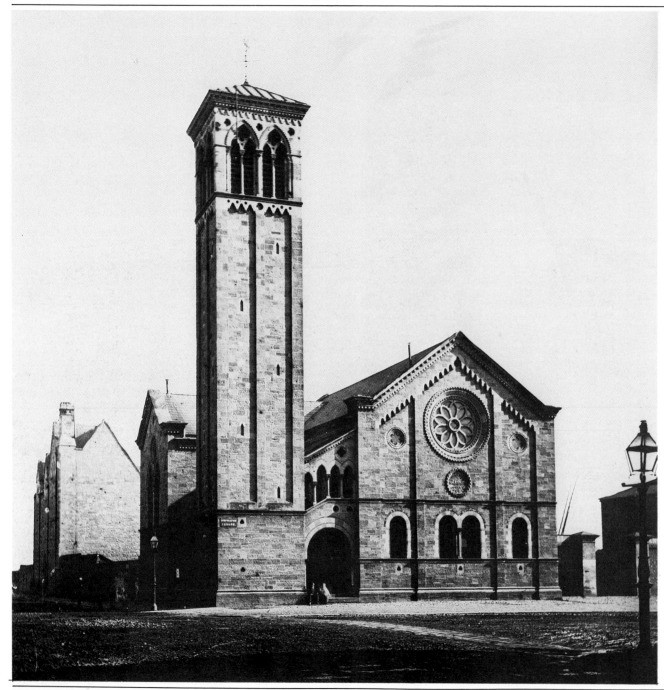

SINCLAIR SEAMEN'S PRESBYTERIAN CHURCH

Just to the west of the Harbour Office at the junction of Corporation Square and Corporation Street is Sinclair Seamen's Church. The foundation stone was laid in October 1857 by Lord Moncrieff, Lord Advocate of Scotland, and it was officially opened for worship by Dr Thomas Guthrie of Edinburgh. The Scottish interest, no doubt, reflected the large proportion of Scottish presbyterian seamen who were expected to use the church while in Belfast. The church replaced an interdenominational chapel in Pilot Street which had been built in 1832 by the Seamen's Friendly Society; presbyterian control came in 1848. The new church was built in his memory by the family of John Sinclair, who died in 1856, with the intention that it 'be considered as specially called on to watch over the spiritual interest of seamen frequenting the port'.[1]

Under the current influence of John Ruskin, the firm of Lanyon and Lynn designed the church to appear Venetian, with a mixture of southern Romanesque and northern gothic elements. The main church is L-shaped and the campanile tower stands in the angle and at the corner of the road junction as if advertising in all directions. The tower is not purely ornamental for it contains a staircase which gives access across a little Bridge-of-Sighs to the gallery of the church. To the left of the church, a little along Corporation Street, can be seen the Sailors' Home which was built at the same time. This photograph was taken before 1865 when railings were erected in front of the church.

The church had at least its fair share of officiating officers with individual characteristics. The first sexton used language which 'it must be acknowledged was not always in accordance with strict ecclesiastical usage'. An early precentor proved to have such a limited range of psalm tunes that the church committee intimated to him that greater variety was imperative: if this was not achieved 'a more unpleasant remedy' might be necessary. The most progressive of its ministers was the Rev. Samuel Cochrane, B.A., R.N., who gave the interior a nautical flavour by installing for the sailors such homely items as the bows and the bowsprit and figurehead of the *Mispah* as a pulpit, with port and starboard lights overhead.[2]

HARBOUR COMMISSIONERS' OFFICES

Back towards the Lagan 'the Harbour Office on the North side of Corporation Square, where the financial and executive business of the port is conducted, is one of the most handsome public buildings in Belfast. It is of white freestone, and surmounted by a light and graceful clock-tower and campanile. It was built after a peculiarly chaste design by G. Smith, Esq., the harbour engineer'.

The new office, begun in 1852 and opened in 1854, replaced one which was both too small and less conveniently placed up river. The site had once been the ship-building yard of William Ritchie; this had a dock which was filled to make Corporation Square. Like many of the mid-century public buildings in Belfast that were concerned with trade or commerce, the model for the architecture was the renaissance palaces of Italy, homes of many of the great merchants and financiers of early modern Europe in the 15th and 16th centuries. As if it were standing in Florence, the Harbour Office has a heavily rusticated ground floor and a more decorative and refined principal floor above. The main entrance, seen here on the left, had an attached portico which faced onto Corporation Square. The long eastern elevation on the right faced across the Clarendon Dock, to the mouth of the Lagan.

Beyond the Office, standing to its west can be seen some four-storey warehouses; these were removed between 1890 and 1895 when the Harbour Office was greatly extended. The eastern elevation and the 'graceful clock-tower and campanile' survive more or less as seen here.

LAGAN NAVIGATION AND RIVER

In 1794 the Lagan navigation stretched from Belfast to Lough Neagh. It began in Belfast at a tidal lock at Stranmillis. Loaded lighters (or barges) were towed by tug boats to Stranmillis from the quays at the Queen's Bridge. Empty boats were usually poled by their crews on the way back. A towpath from Stranmillis to Lough Neagh allowed the boats to be drawn all the way by horse. Development of the railways affected the traffic on the canal but until the first world war, over 100,000 tons of cargo were carried annually. Further competition from motor lorry transport in the 1920s led to the closure of the canal[1] Regrettably, sections of the canal were allowed to fall into disrepair and are no longer navigable.

The view on the left is at Stranmillis at the very beginning of the Lagan navigation. Belfast Boat Club was built in the late 1890s to the right of the cottage[2] In the picture one can see a number of wooden clinker-built open boats, including one double-ender, alongside the river bank. A metal-hull, river cruise-steamer is in the background. The photograph on the right shows some lighters on the Lagan river adjacent to the Queen's Bridge. There are also more double-ended clinker-built open boats in the water. The masts and spars of sailing colliers can be observed at the Queen's Quay on the downstream side of the bridge. The large building on the left just beyond the bridge is the Custom House.

The Queen's Bridge, opened in 1842, was the outcome of a joint resolution of the Grand Juries of Down and Antrim to demolish the old Long Bridge, erected in 1682, and build a new one, suitable for the greatly increased traffic. 'This has been done, with great skill and elegance of design, by Mr Lanyon, at an expense of £20,000. A stroll along this bridge will amply repay the visitor. It commands some of the most pleasing views of the city and environs, embracing the river, with its fleet of steamers and merchant vessels, the magnificent range of quays, with their characteristic groups engaged in all the bustle of mercantile activity; and beyond this busy scene, stretching away behind the city, and skirting the harbour towards Carrickfergus, the mountains form a background of singular interest and beauty'[3]

THE BANGOR BOAT

The first steamer to operate between Belfast and Bangor was the *Greenock* which arrived in Belfast in April 1816. Her appearance had clearly a startling effect as some citizens of Belfast, who had never seen a steamer before, thought she was on fire. A number of trips to Bangor were organised in that year on the *Greenock* and later in the mid-1820s on the *Bangor Castle*. A regular service, however, was established only in the early 1850s.

These two photographs, taken probably in the late 1870s, are of the P.S. *Erin*. Launched at Port Glasgow in June 1864, the *Erin* was a two-funnelled vessel which was capable of going from Belfast to Bangor in 40 minutes. Contemporary reports commented favourably on her internal furnishings. In 1890, the *Erin* was involved in an accident with another Bangor steamer, the *Victoria*. Keen competition between the two boats had led to a race from Belfast to Bangor during which the boats collided, although with little damage. Both captains were arrested and fined!

The photograph on the left shows the *Erin* approaching the Queen's Bridge jetty. In the foreground on the right there are a number of sailing colliers, chiefly brigantines, moored off or discharging at Queen's Quay. To the left of the *Erin* in the distance there are various cross-channel steamers alongside Donegall Quay while beyond them can be seen the masts and spars of square-rigged sailing vessels engaged in the foreign trade. Note the large numbers of people on board the *Erin*. At the time of the accident in 1890 she was carrying 500 passengers. The view on the right shows the *Erin* moored at the Queen's Bridge jetty.

THE BANGOR BOAT

The above view is of the P.S. *Bangor Castle*. Built in 1864 by Wingate of Glasgow, the steamer began the Belfast-Bangor route in 1873. Originally called the *Palmerston*, the name was changed to *Bangor Castle* in 1877 after she was re-registered in Belfast. Besides the trip to Bangor, the steamer sometimes sailed to Larne or Donaghadee. She was sold to the Plymouth Excursion Steam Boat Co. and left the lough in 1894. The *Bangor Castle* was scrapped in 1899!

The photograph on the back cover shows the steamer at Queen's Bridge jetty. In the background at Donegall Quay cross channel shipping can be seen. On the extreme right is the P.S. *Erin*. The photograph above is the *Bangor Castle* probably *en route* for Bangor.

NOTES AND PLATE NUMBERS

ABBREVIATIONS

These abbreviations are used for the most commonly cited mid-nineteenth century sources:—

Thackeray, *Irish sketch book*	W. M. Thackeray, *The Irish sketch book of 1842* (London, 1877)
Hall, *Ireland*	Mr and Mrs S. C. Hall, *Ireland: its scenery, character . . .vol. III* (London, 1843)
Huband Smith, *Belfast*	J. Huband Smith, *Belfast and its environs*, (Dublin, 2nd edition 1853)
Doyle, *Tours*	J. B. Doyle, *Tours in Ulster, a hand book to the antiquities & scenery . . .* (Dublin, 1854)
McComb's guide	W. McComb, *McComb's guide to Belfast, the Giant's Causeway, and adjoining districts . . .* (Belfast, 1861)

Also frequently cited are:—

Brett, *Belfast*	C. E. B. Brett, *Buildings of Belfast 1700-1914* (London, 1967)
Walker and Dixon, *No mean city*	B. M. Walker and Hugh Dixon, *No mean city: Belfast 1880-1914 in the photographs of Robert French* (Belfast, 1983)

CATALOGUE NUMBERS

The numbers quoted beside the plate titles refer to the catalogue numbers of the original glass negatives in the Lawrence Stereograph Collection in the National Library of Ireland, Dublin.

Front Cover. Donegall Place   2513

Page 2. High Street   2499

Introduction

1. B. M. Walker, *Shadows on glass: a portfolio of early Ulster photography* (Belfast, 1976) p.6 (hereafter cited as Walker, *Shadows*); Edward Chandler, *Photography in Dublin during the Victorian era* (Dublin, n.d.) p.2.
2. Durham Dunlop, *A memoir of the professional life of W. J. Barre Esq* (Belfast, 1868) (hereafter cited as Dunlop, *Barre*).
3. E. D. Hill, *The Northern Bank: an historical sketch, 1824-1924* (Belfast, 1925).
4. Kieran Hickey (ed.), *The light of other days: Irish life at the turn of the century in the photographs of Robert French* (London, 1973) pp9-16.
5. C. E. B. Brett, 'The Georgian town: Belfast about 1800' in J. C. Beckett and R. E. Glasscock (eds), *Belfast: the origin and growth of an industrial city* (Belfast, 1967), p.67; W. E. Vaughan and A. J. Fitzpatrick (eds), *Irish historical statistics: population 1821-1971* (Dublin, 1978), pp 36-7.
6. W. M. O'Hanlon, *Walks among the poor of Belfast* (Belfast, 1853).
7. Hall, *Ireland*, p. 53.

Page 3. Fountain in the Crystal Palace, Queen's Island   385
1. Jim Patton, 'William Dargan and his island' in *East Belfast Post*, 29 Mar 1984, p.8.
2. John Gray, 'Popular entertainment' in J. C. Beckett et al, *Belfast: the making of the city 1800-1914* (Belfast, 1982) pp 101-2.
3. Reproduced in Arthur Deane (ed.) *The Belfast Natural History and Philosophical Society, centenary volume, 1821-1921* (Belfast, 1924) p. 30.

Page 8. Ulster Railway Terminus, Great Victoria Street   376
1. W. A. McCutcheon in *Ulster Journal of Archaeology*, 3rd series, XXVII, 1964, 159.
2. *Proceedings of the Institution of Civil Engineers*, XXX, 1869-70, pp 434-5.
3. W. A. McCutcheon, *The industrial archaeology of Northern Ireland* (Belfast, 1980), p. 172, plate 25; Walker and Dixon, *No mean city*, p. 36.

Page 9. Fisherwick Place Presbyterian Church   451
1. Huband Smith, *Belfast*, pp 34-5; *A history of congregations in the Presbyterian Church in Ireland, 1610-1982* (Belfast, 1982) (hereafter cited as *Presbyterian congregations*), p. 165.
2. Thackeray, *Irish sketch book*, p. 508.
3. Walker and Dixon, *No mean city*, pp 32, 33, 50.

Pages 10 and 11. Statues of the Earl of Belfast and the Rev. Henry Cooke College Square East   386 and 1993
1. 'Frederick Richard, Earl of Belfast, 1827-1853' in *Belfast Municipal Gallery and Museum: quarterly notes*, LV, no. 119, Dec. 1937, pp 10-15
2. Brett, *Belfast*, 47-8; Walker and Dixon, *No mean city*, p. 31.

Page 12. The Museum, College Square North   449
1. Arthur Deane (ed.), *The Belfast Natural History and Philosophical Society centenary volume, 1821-1921* (Belfast, 1924) p. 6 and passim.
2. Hugh Dixon, 'Honouring Thomas Jackson' in *Proceedings of the Belfast Natural History and Philosophical Society*, Vol. 9 1978, pp 23-25.
3. Noel Nesbitt, *A museum in Belfast: a history of the Ulster Museum and its predecessors* (Belfast, 1979).
4. *Belfast directories*, 1861, 1892.

Page 13. Christ Church, College Square North   452
1. John Gray, 'Popular entertainment' in *Belfast: the making of the city* (Belfast, 1982) p. 100.
2. *McComb's guide*, p. 23.
3. Brett, *Belfast*, p. 19.

Page 14. Bedford Street from Donegall Square   1983
1. Brett, *Belfast*, p. 59.
2. *Belfast directories*, 1850s and 1860s.
3. *The Builder*, 17 April 1852, pp 245-6.
4. *Irish Builder*, 15 September 1869, p. 213.

Page 15. The Ulster Hall, Bedford Street   383
1. Dunlop, *Barre*, pp 22-24 and unpaginated section turn 14 & 15.
2. *McComb's guide*, p. 29.
3. Walker and Dixon, *No mean city*, pp 38-9.

Page 16. The Queen's College, University Road   439
1. See T. W. Moody, 'Higher education' in T. W. Moody and J. C. Beckett (eds), *Ulster since 1800: second series, a social survey* (London, 1957) pp 95-9.
2. Doyle, *Tours*, p.34.

Page 17. Elmwood Presbyterian Church, University Road   381.
1. James Dewar, *A history of Elmwood Presbyterian Church* (Belfast, 1900)
2. Brett, *Belfast*, p. 36; Hugh Dixon, *Ulster architecture 1800-1900* (Belfast, 1972) p. 19.
3. S. T. Carleton, 'The growth of South Belfast' (M.A. thesis, 1967, The Queen's University of Belfast; hereafter cited as Carleton, *South Belfast*) p. 114.

Page 18. Deaf and Dumb Institute from Elmwood Avenue   382
1. Carleton, *South Belfast*, p. 114; Hugh Dixon and David Evans, *Historic buildings . . . in the vicinity of Queen's University* (Belfast, 1975) p. 27.

Page 19. Deaf and Dumb Institute, Lisburn Road   441
1. J. Kinghan in *Quarterly Review of Deaf-Mute Education*, Jan.-Apr. 1891, pp 4-9.
2. Doyle, *Tours*, p. 38.

Page 20. Fitzroy Avenue Presbyterian Church   1989
1. R. E. Alexander, *Fitzroy Avenue Presbyterian Church: past and present* (Belfast, 1949) pp 18-19.
2. Carleton, *South Belfast*, p. 141; Dixon and Evans, *Historic buildings . . . Queens*, p. 17.

Page 21. Alfred Street Presbyterian Church   455
1. *Presbyterian congregations*, pp 166-7.
2. R. E. Alexander, *Fitzroy Avenue Presbyterian Church*, pp 11-14.

Page 22. St Malachy's Catholic Church   457
1. *St. Malachy's Church, Belfast: centenary record* (Belfast, 1948) pp 4-11.
2. Brett, *Belfast*, 23; Hugh Dixon in *Proceedings Belfast Natural History Society*, Vol. 9, 1978, p. 25; Thackeray, *Irish sketch book*, p. 508.

Page 23. May Street Presbyterian Church   454
1. Brett, *Belfast*, pp 17-18; Hall, *Ireland*, p. 58; J. Williamson, *Centenary history* (Belfast, 1929).
2. Doyle, *Tours*, p. 32.
3. *McComb's guide*, pp 24-5.
4. *The Builder*, 11 September 1858, p. 615.
5. *Belfast directories*, 1849 and later.

Page 24. Music Hall, May Street   448
1. *McComb's guide*, p. 29.
2. Brett, *Belfast*, p. 23.
3. *Belfast Commercial Chronicle*, 2 January 1843, p. 4.

Page 25. Donegall Square Methodist Church   462
1. *Donegall Square Methodist Church—a centenary record 1950* (Belfast, 1950); Brett, *Belfast*, p. 23.
2. Thackeray, *Irish sketch book*, p. 508.

Page 26. White Linen Hall, Donegall Square   1990
1. Huband Smith, *Belfast*, p. 56.
2. C. E. B. Brett, *Roger Mulholland, architect of Belfast, 1740-1818* (Belfast, 1976).
3. *Black's guide to Belfast* (Edinburgh, 1872) (hereafter cited as *Black's guide*) p. 334.

Page 27. Donegall Place and the Royal Hotel   2496
1. Walker and Dixon, *No mean city*, pp 14-15.
2. *Industries of Ireland: part 1: Belfast and the towns of the north* (London, 1891) p. 93.
3. Thackeray, *Irish sketch book*, 507-8.
4. *Industries of Ireland . . .*, p. 93.

Page 28. Castle Place   2506 or 2497
1. *Belfast directory*, 1877, p. 369.

Page 29. Theatre Royal, Arthur Square   1987
1. *Irish Builder*, 15 October 1871, pp 262-3.
2. Se John Gray, 'Popular entertainment' in *Belfast: the making of the city* (Belfast, 1982) pp 107-8.
3. *Irish Builder*, 15 September 1871, p. 245.

Pages 30 and 31. Victoria Street from Jaffe Fountain, and from Chichester Street 1988 and 2495
1. Walker and Dixon, *No mean city*, pp 12-13.
2. *Irish Builder*, 1 Feb 1868, p. 33; T. Jackson and Sons, architects.
3. *The Builder*, XXVIII, 1870, pp 286, 400.

Page 32. Northern Bank, Victoria Street   443
1. *The Builder*, IX, 1851, p. 679; X, 1852, p. 537.
2. Brett, *Belfast*, p. 30 and plate 32.
3. *McComb's guide*, p. 33.

Page 33. Ulster Bank, Waring Street   444
1. *McComb's guide*, p. 33; *Decades of the Ulster Bank 1836-1964* (Belfast, 1965) p. 70.
2. Dunlop, *Barre*, unpaginated section turn 4-7 from end.
3. Brett, *Belfast*, pp 32, 37.
4. *Dublin Builder*, 1 June 1859, p. 66; *Irish Builder*, 1 October 1869, p. 220.

Page 34. St Anne's Church, Donegall Street   460
1. Huband Smith, *Belfast*, pp 41-43.
2. Hall, *Ireland*, p. 57.
3. *McComb's guide*, p. 22.

Page 35. St Patrick's Church, Donegall Street   458
1. *Belfast Newsletter*, 7 March 1815; Fred Heatley, *The story of St. Patrick's, Belfast, 1815-1977* (Belfast, 1977) pp 13 and 46.
2. Thackeray, *Irish sketch book*, p. 508.
3. Walker and Dixon, *No mean city*, p. 74.

Pages 36 and 37. Custom House   445, 447 and 1986
1. Hugh Dixon, *Ulster architecture 1800-1900* (Belfast, 1972) p. 26; Brett, *Belfast*, pp 29-30.
2. *McComb's guide*, pp 32-3.
3. Walker and Dixon, *No mean city*, p. 92, and for the GPO p. 66.

Page 38. Sinclair Seamen's Presbyterian Church   450
1. *Sinclair Seaman's Presbyterian Church, souvenir booklet* (Glasgow, 1957) p. 4.
2. Brett, *Belfast*, p. 30.

Page 39. Harbour Commissioners' Offices   446
1. *McComb's guide*, p. 19.
2. Brett, *Belfast*, p. 29; Walker and Dixon, *No mean city*, p. 90.

Pages 40 and 41. Lagan Navigation and River   387   2496
1. D. B. McNeill, *Coastal passenger steamers and inland navigation in the north of Ireland* (Belfast, 1960; 2nd impression 1967) pp 18-19.
2. See Walker and Dixon, *No mean city*, p. 49.
3. Doyle, *Tours*, p. 31.

Pages 42 and 43. The Bangor Boat   2576   2514
1. D. B. McNeill, *Irish passenger steamship services: volume 1, north of Ireland* (Newton Abbot, 1969) pp 137-45.

Page 44 and Cover. The Bangor Boat   1992   2514
1. D. B. McNeill, *Irish passenger steamship services . . .*, pp 137-45.

Page 47. St John's Church, Laganbank   456
1. *Parish of Saint John the Evangelist, Orangefield: 21 years of church extension in Castlereagh* (Belfast, 1957) pp 17-19; the church is visible on J. H. Connop's bird's-eye view of 1860 (available in Linen Hall Library).

Page 48 Model School, Falls Road   442
1. *McComb's guide*, pp 27-8; A. R. Craig and Norman McNeilly, *Belfast Model Schools, 1857-1957* (Belfast, 1957).

Index

Bold type denotes plate titles

ST JOHN'S CHURCH OF IRELAND CHURCH, LAGANBANK

Built in 1853, St John's was a good example of mid-Victorian gothic revival style of a fairly unelaborate type. It had no very dominant vertical feature such as tower or spire, only a simple bell gable at the west end, and not even a bell. Nevertheless it was a large building with six full coupled bays of windows in both main nave and lower aisles, and each of the three parts had its own richly carved and deeply recessed portico. A chimney at the east end marked the site of the vestry.

Known popularly as 'St John's in the mud', it was built on a rather isolated site on the Laganbank Road, at the extreme, eastern projection of May Street, adjacent to what became the Albert Bridge. It was believed that a population would develop on the Oxford Street side of the church. This never happened and the area was built over by warehouses and business premises. The church, with railway track to one side and the Corporation store yard on the other, then survived until 1943 when it was demolished. The existing endowments and furnishings passed to St John's, Orangefield.

ACKNOWLEDGEMENTS

We wish to thank all who have helped with this book. Special thanks are due to Mr Michael O'Connell of R.T.E., Dublin, who informed us about these stereographic views. We are grateful to the National Library of Ireland for permission to reproduce the photographs. Special gratitude is owed to Mr Eugene Hogan for his excellent prints. Mr Michael McCaughan of the Ulster Folk Museum provided valuable information on the ship photographs. We also gratefully acknowledge help from the Linen Hall Library, the Ulster Museum and the Historic Monuments and Buildings Branch, DoENI. Finally, many thanks are due to Mr Charles Brett.

MODEL SCHOOL, FALLS ROAD

West from College Square, near where Divis Street bends southwards to become the Falls Road, stood the District Model School, opened in 1857. Building costs of £14,000 seem large by mid-Victorian standards, but the school was more extensive than this photograph of the main front might suggest. The building was as deep as it was wide and built around a central light well. During the 1860s the school had an average attendance of 1,100!

Contemporary accounts of the building describe its style as 'Tudor', a term too broadly used to cover the revival of building styles of the sixteenth and seventeenth centuries. The school had some 'Tudor' features such as the windows but with its rigid symmetry and curving gables its character is predominantly 'Jacobean'. The doorway looks more 'Baroque'. Thus the style is a typical High Victorian mixture of historic styles all of which have appropriate Oxbridge collegiate associations.

Belfast Model School was one of a number of model schools established in the mid-nineteenth century by the Board of Commissioners of National Education. Their purpose was to be a model of what should be aimed at in the national system and they were to be non-denominational. Another aim was to train teachers for the national schools. They provided a wide curriculum which included practical subjects such as bookkeeping and agriculture.

The Belfast school was initially successful in attracting pupils from all denominations but catholic objections to the system from the late 1860s led to a drop in the proportion of catholics. By the last decades of the nineteenth century the school was almost entirely protestant. The building was destroyed by incendiary devices in 1922. Temporary school facilities were established at Cliftonville and eventually two new model schools, providing secondary education, were built at Oldpark and Ballysillan.